ALAÏA

First published in Great Britain in 1996 by
Thames and Hudson Ltd, London

Copyright © 1996 Editions Assouline, Paris

British Library Cataloguing-in-Publication Data
A catalogue record for this book is available from the British Library
ISBN 0-500-01719-0

Printed and bound in Italy

ALAÏA

Text by François Baudot

THAMES AND HUDSON

'On its journey through history, love preserves intact the events it touches.'

Louise de Vilmorin.

this characteristically direct and pertinent statement – the first line of Louise de Vilmorin's novel *Madame de ...* – could equally well have been applied to fashion as to love. Indeed, the two make good bedfellows, each looking to the other in times of trouble. And yet the number of fashion designers a woman could name as having left a distinctive impression on her life – including her love life – are few and far between. The latter half of this century will have witnessed the style of Chanel, the glory of Christian Dior, passion according to Saint Laurent, and the unfailing promise of Christian Lacroix. After this, however, things become rather more hazy, at least as far as the general public is concerned. But there is an increasing number of initiates, both men and women, who are becoming aware of one phenomenon in particular – Azzedine Alaïa. The word Alaïa, partly magical, partly a rallying cry, redefines time in terms of what came before and what came after. Initially whispered in hushed tones, then repeated, the word unlocks the secrets of a new kind of elegance which is more to do with the way clothes are worn than with the clothes them-

5

selves. Like Dr Cornelius, the mysterious and diabolical hero in the novels of Gustave le Rouge, Alaïa sculpts human flesh from the depths of his lair, reconstructing the female figure by correcting imperfections and emphasizing existing qualities. He combines violence, modesty and eroticism by hinting at a woman's desirable attributes while keeping them out of reach – the essence of the Oriental.

So where did Alaïa come from, and when and how did his story really begin? To attempt to trace back the turbulent course of his life would be like trying to find the source of the Nile. It is a story in which the only reality seems to be the dresses themselves. The unique place he occupies in the codified world of fashion is one that only he could feel comfortable with, running the gamut between unselfconscious haute couture and the occasional ready-to-wear collection, as well as being a truly great tailor. His status oscillates between that of the best tailors in Savile Row and that of the domestic dressmaker, and between the elegance of a bygone era and the passing whim of a young girl who no sooner has one thing than is on to the next.

And yet, ever since he learned how to sew, and discovered new materials and the tricks of cutting, Alaïa has completely transformed the figures of those who had faith in him. Many other designers have been influenced by him unawares, not to mention outright copyists. Like Ali Baba, Alaïa had forty thieves, who owed their success largely to him. It was purely on the strength of his own ideas, however, that Alaïa achieved success, completely disregarding the time in which he lived. Thus, after over thirty years loyal service in the business, Alaïa still gives the impression – without even having to cultivate this image – of being a worthy struggling designer in need of being pushed, protected and encouraged. He is the opposite of those who are primarily concerned with the completed product, being interested only in beginning – a new dress or a new affair. The only endings he enjoys are the finishing touches, though his finest designs are those which are created by just two snips of the scissors – fluid motion suspended in time and space with just a few pins: the second skin of a perfect body.

Alaïa's world has its own laws and customs which have evolved during the course of his life. In the beginning he worked in a maid's room crammed full of his female friends, many of them models even at this stage. He then moved to an apartment which wealthy ladies visited surreptitiously between five and seven o'clock, cheating on their regular couturiers. Today, the House of Alaïa occupies an entire block which used to house a warehouse, the local school and a hothouse. Inside it looks like a cross between an Alexandre Trauner set design for a Marcel Carné film and a high-tech New York loft. Some 3,000 square metres house the boutique, studio, storerooms, workshops, lumber rooms, catwalk, show rooms, dormitory, fitting rooms, canteen and even a private bedroom. The 'bedroom' consists of a mattress on the floor set among a rare African sculpture, a monumental canvas by Julian Schnabel, a bundle of sweaters just in from Italy and some portfolios full of loose photographs, prints, original drawings, gouaches and so on. From this apparently disordered jumble Alaïa unearths any reference material he needs, including his collection of contemporary artwork, which is as remarkable as it is eclectic. But the main focus of the House of Alaïa is the studio, a long glass room which has seen some of the most famous and beautiful women in the world. Here, sitting behind his sturdy cutting table, Alaïa looks even tinier than usual. As well as being his sketchbook and laboratory, his table doubles as his headquarters and sometimes even his bed. Late at night, having strained his eyes from cutting out and sewing countless designs ready for the following day, he would curl up like a cat on an off-cut of silk and no doubt dream that the beautiful dress hanging up before him was winging its way to a princess who, in her gratitude, would shower him with gold.

a laïa discovered the secrets of dressmaking by collecting and examining in detail both period clothing and dresses by his favourite couturiers, who include Madeleine Vionnet and Balenciaga. He perceived the construction of clothes through the centuries to be a science about which he intended to know everything. This knowledge, combined with his imagination, forms the foundations for his unique skill which, when it is adapted to the demands of the modern woman and to new manufacturing processes and materials, results in the incomparable Alaïa style. His designs are both modern and timeless, personal and neutral. At times they might seem to verge on the ordinary were it not for the fact that in the blink of an eye, when he came to prominence in the eighties, he rendered whole areas of fashion obsolete.

Alaïa was born in Tunis, which makes him, if not a true Frenchman, then at least a true Parisian. He always wore a silk or sateen Chinese jacket, of which he possessed hundreds, a pair of dark trousers and velvet slippers. Everything about him was black, including his mischievous eyes, his curly hair and his clothes – everything, that is, except his youthful mind which was stimulated by the slightest thing, jumping from one idea to another, fascinated by everything around him.

As a boy in Tunisia Alaïa was small for his age, but he had dreams and knew that one day he would get to Paris and be successful. His first calling was as a sculptor so his grandmother, who had raised him, enrolled him at the Ecole des Beaux-Arts and his life as an artist began. Today perhaps the history of art would have claimed another sculptor had it not been for Madame Pineau. She was the local midwife, but she had a penchant for fashion magazines which she kept in her clinic, and it was here that Alaïa worked as her assistant, heating water and bringing towels.

fascinated and terrified by the births he witnessed, Alaïa learned at an early age to respect and care for the female body. Its workings, attractions and strengths gradually convinced him that his place would always be with women. Between deliveries, punctuated by the babies' cries, the apprentice sculptor/midwife would immerse himself in the Parisian magazines. He admired the beautiful dresses and the women, who seemed so different from those he saw every day. They convinced him of his true vocation – he would continue to sculpt them, but in the flesh, using fabric rather than in marble.

When he finally received permission from his grandfather to go to Paris, Alaïa went to work at Christian Dior's, where he stayed just five days. The Algerian War had broken out and a young Arab boy was not welcome. In any case, Alaïa did not want to work for a clientele like Dior's. It was while he was under the protection of one of his compatriots, Simone Zehrfuss, the beautiful wife of the great architect Bernard Zehrfuss, that he was initiated into a more elegant world. After two seasons working for the couturier Guy Laroche, he went to stay with the Comtesse de Blégiers in the avenue Victor Hugo in the smart sixteenth arrondissement of Paris. Here he looked after her children and helped with the cooking, devoting the rest of his time to his first efforts at dress design. In this safe haven he felt perfectly happy, particularly since he came to meet and admire and finally design clothes for such exceptional women as Louise de Vilmorin, Greta Garbo, Cécile de Rothschild and Arletty.

right up until the end of her life, the actress Arletty remained his friend and confidante. Although she became blind, she remained as lively and alluring as ever – she came to symbolize a certain style and a particular type for the designer. She would have thought of herself 'un sacré type', but he preferred to see her as a true Parisian, a child of the people, who could teach aristocratic ladies a thing or two.

When Alaïa took four rooms in the rue de Bellechasse on the modest first floor his bohemian lifestyle came to an end. Here, employing a few workers, he spent years creating made-to-measure clothes – working to a punishing schedule – for a discreet and elegant clientele who heard of him by word of mouth. The mischievous tailor, of course, took risks with his more daring customers. To show off their figures, he particularly emphasized the small of the back and the buttocks.

alaïa excels at bringing out the physical qualities in a girl of sixteen that will make her a great model, a star or a personality, revealing her beauty hidden behind an often timid exterior and misconceived self-image. Naomi Campbell, the first black top model to appear in international magazines, remains, above all the others, the most exciting of his discoveries. He dresses and even undresses her, with the same skill as he used to make the fifties model and film star Bettina look more seductive than ever in the nineties in figure-hugging mesh and a little felted wool suit.

When Alaïa the alchemist went into fashion, he became interested in materials – as much in manufacturing processes as in whether or not a garment was cut on the bias. He uses flowing fabrics which yield to the touch, discovering new materials such as Lycra and repopularizing neglected ones such as viscose. The stretchy figure-hugging dresses and skin-tight tops and leggings, which can be seen everywhere in the high street today, were originally his creation. They bring together the sexy and the comfortable.

It was due to the support of a few fashion editors, some informed stylists and faithful friends such as the designer Thierry Mugler, as well as to the trends of the late seventies, that the little tailor was finally forced into the public eye. In 1979, Alaïa created a raincoat and a ready-to-wear suit for Madeleine Furs. Modest beginnings perhaps, but they were instantly picked up by *Elle* and photographed. Others followed.

the first Alaïa collections arrived in 1980. The designer presented them at his apartment – he made no concessions, with no invitations and no music. People fought over kitchen stools; the bathroom doubled up as a make-up room. All fashionable Paris wanted to be there and many who were not boasted about having been the first to discover the eighth wonder of the fashion world. In Paris, news travels by word of mouth – a means of communication Alaïa mastered so well that he did not need to advertise. In the eighties, the press included Alaïa, somewhat against his will, in a movement christened 'the young designers' (although youth is a fault that is rectified with each passing day). As well as receiving unwavering support from a few journalists including Michel Cressole from *La Libération*, Nicole Crassat, and Melka Treanton from *Elle*, Alaïa became known to a much wider public due to a commission from Maïmé Arnodin and Denise Fayolle. These two advisers to the French textile industry and great fashion oracles asked Alaïa to create a nice skirt to be sold at a low price for the very popular mail-order catalogue *Les 3 Suisses*. All over Paris and on the backs of buses the close-up photograph of a model's backside in Alaïa's figure-hugging skirt was the source of many a male fantasy. Similarly in 1995 he designed a dress for another popular catalogue, *La Redoute*, which was posted up on billboards everywhere, modelled by a beautiful voluptuous girl photographed next to the impish, smiling figure of Alaïa himself, in his ever-present black jacket.

As well as receiving popular acclaim, Alaïa also attracted a private and select clientele whom he would see to personally, down to the last detail. This clientele included Tina Turner, Madonna, supermodels and film stars – they would come to Alaïa's in secret for an afternoon when they wanted their morale lifted, among other things. The beautiful Stephanie Seymour even chose the illuminated glass-roofed House of Alaïa rather than the Ritz for her fairy-tale wedding celebrations.

But it was to be at the 1985 Fashion Oscars at the Opéra in Paris that Alaïa achieved his widest recognition yet. Present at the ceremony, which was shown live on French television, was the President's wife, Madame François Mitterand, who, as it transpired, had for a long time been a regular customer at the House of Alaïa. To his amazement, Alaïa, the outcast and ugly duckling of Hans Andersen's tale, found himself the recipient of two Oscars awarded in recognition of his entire career; a career which he himself felt to be just beginning. Had he even wanted such fame?

In his designs Alaïa eschews all incidental detail, that old adversary of elegance. He generally uses neutral colours such as black, beige, navy, taupe, subtle pastels and off-whites, and he presents his designs without jewelry and with few accessories. Using neither gaudy baubles nor assumed austerity, he has capitalized instead on the seductiveness of a woman's curvaceous figure, which he wants to appear as feminine rather than overtly sexy. With his creation of the famous 'body' perfected in the early eighties and worn by thousands of women, Alaïa literally transformed the way women moved. In the late twentieth century, this stretch fabric will have done for Alaïa what jersey did for Chanel at the beginning of her career – it will have caused a gentle but irreversible revolution. By doing away with lining, making the clothes as light as possible and emphasizing the figure, stretchy fabric unites form and movement to create a new structure for the body which is in perfect harmony with contemporary tastes.

Traditionally, a dress is fitted from the shoulders and a skirt from the waist – they hang, or rather 'fall', from these points with varying degrees of success depending on the talent of the designer and the quality of the garment. What Alaïa did, however, was to create clothes which cling, such as his dress made of bound strips. While following the body's slightest movements, it still manages to retain its original shape. In this way a woman, as a living sculpture, embodies the synthesis of Alaïa's two vocations as sculptor and fashion designer. Continuing his re-creation of the body and his study of the female form, more recently Alaïa has embarked on the restoration of the 'balcony' bra using updated and redesigned corsetry which highlights, even accentuates, the bust. Taking into account that the majority of women spend much of their time sitting down, whether in the office, at the cinema or the theatre, at a table or in the car, the designer concentrates entirely on the part of the body which is most visible in this position (what used to be known in French as 'la gorge').

a laïa is less interested in fashion itself than in the desires of other people, thus marketing is second nature to him. His designs, founded on a fascination for love and an interest in other people, are a pretext for social interaction. Most of all, Alaïa likes to meet important women, and beautiful women. The men – both seductive and seduced – follow in their wake. These include painters, writers and actors, who all end up, as do the objects of their desire, at Alaïa's – the one stable point in this shifting world of seduction. The New York artist Julian Schnabel met Alaïa at the various fittings of his successive partners, forming such a close friendship with him that, at the end of the eighties, he decorated Alaïa's new shop in New York. He also helped to fit out his warehouse in the rue de Moussy where the designer set up his artistic and commercial venture. It is undoubtedly the only fashion house entirely conceived by a great contemporary artist for no payment. In the shop-cum-studio, lording over two columns sculpted by Schnabel, a Dogon hut post, some dresses (of course), and a few handbags, is an enlarged monumental bronze cast of a woman's bust by the sculptor César, another great friend of the designer, along with a few Art Deco chairs, some Baule masks, a Jean Prouvé table and a Fortuny lamp.

Farida, like Alaïa, was born on the Mediterranean coast. For a long time her untamed beauty and perfect body made her not only his favourite model, whom he used for close to ten years to base his main collections on, but also his confidante at work. The fashion world called her his muse, but he preferred to call her his friend. She was the one who introduced him to the inventive Jean-Paul Goude. Each as passionate as the other about the reconstruction of the human anatomy, they struck up a friendship based on a genuine shared interest which resulted in close collaboration. They worked together on videos and publicity shots, and the unforgettable fashion extravaganza 'La Marseillaise' which brought to a close the bicentenary celebrations of the French Revolution on 14 July 1989. For this event, Goude involved Alaïa in some of the tableaux that he had scripted, and the designer found himself entrusted with the train of the loose tricolour gown worn by the opera singer Jessie Norman when she sang the national anthem at the foot of la Concorde.

laïa has an equally special relationship with some of the greatest photographers of our time. Like them, he is passionate about his role as an image-maker. Another example of his special relationship with contemporary creative thinking was the exhibition in 1985 at the Museum of Contemporary Art in Bordeaux (the CAPC) dedicated to him by the director, Jean-Louis Froment. The CAPC is one of the most respected centres of the avant-garde in Europe, and here in the exhibition halls a day of films, discussions and continuous fashion shows of ten years of Alaïa's work was staged. It was an exceptional honour for him. That day the entire town, known for its conservatism, shared his particular and innovative ideas on fashion. Top models came from all four corners of the globe and filed past a crowd of international journalists and fans. In a confusion of seasons, years and events, Alaïa's designs

15

whirled by, undatable, unplaceable, dazzling. Never was the master of contemporary elegance so appreciated for his range and exceptional understated skill as he was during this live retrospective. Like a continuing melody, his body of work contains themes which make a complete turn about and develop, which come to the fore, recede and then resurface once again with only the subtlest of changes. Defying the hands of time, Alaïa prizes the constancy of seduction over the trend of the moment to achieve the ultimate aim: beauty.

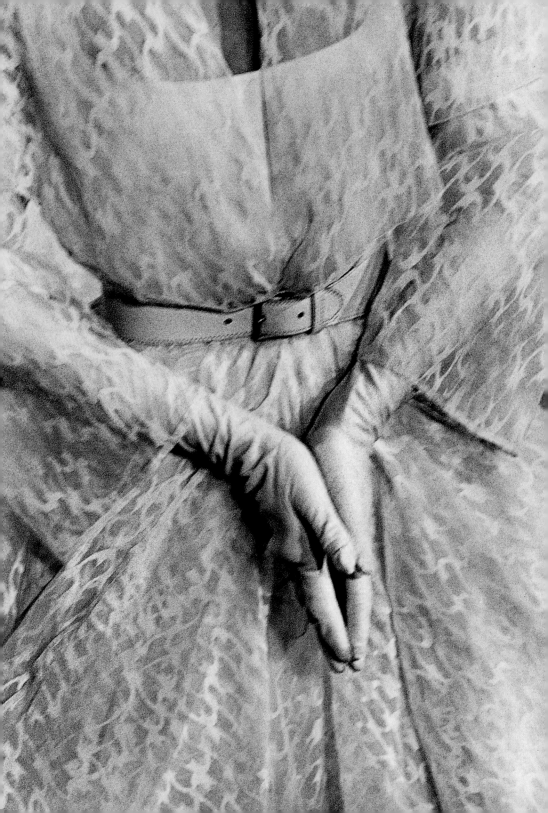

Déesses –

In May 1995, Alaïa created this Arabic hooded cloak as a maternity dress for Farida, his close friend and long-standing model. Photo Jean-Marie Perrier, taken at the Musée National des Arts d'Afrique et d'Océanie, Paris.

Select chronology

Azzedine Alaïa was born in Tunisia. While he was studying sculpture at the Ecole des Beaux-Arts in Tunis, he became interested in fashion and began his career by copying the haute couture designs from Paris for the well-dressed women of the city.

1957   Alaïa arrives in Paris.

Under the recommendation of one of his clients, goes to work for Christian Dior but only stays there for five days.

Works for Guy Laroche for two seasons where he learns the secrets and customs of haute couture and discovers his true vocation.

1960–1970 Little by little, finds his own private clientele due to his contacts in Tunis, and creates made-to-measure clothes.

Thanks to one of his clients, Simone Zehrfuss, the wife of the architect Bernard Zehrfuss, he moves into his first apartment/studio at 60, rue de Bellechasse where he stays until 1984.

Through Simone Zehrfuss, Alaïa meets the poet and novelist Louise de Vilmorin, a witty and learned society woman. He becomes her friend and confidant. She introduces him to the elegant Parisian social scene, expanding and enriching his clientele which was to include, most notably, Arletty.

In a climate of social upheaval, the influence of haute couture was diminishing. During the seventies Alaïa adapts to changing demands by appealing to a younger clientele.

1980   Alaïa gets himself noticed with his design for a waxed tunic with metal eyelets, photographed in *Dépêche Mode*.

From the beginning of the eighties, he concentrates particularly on low-cut, uplifted bodices and garments which are backless and close-fitting, exploiting the properties of new materials.

1981   Alaïa launches his first collection. The *Alaïa* label is created.
Although he invents the 'body' at the beginning of the year, it is not launched until his Autumn/Winter 1981–1982 collection appears.

One of his many revolutionary designs is a black leather suit which is spotted by the press and photographed by a number of international fashion magazines. During the eighties, crowds of journalists, actors and celebrities from all over the world come to his fashion shows which he holds in his apartment.

1982   In New York, the Bergdorf & Goodman chain hold a large scale fashion show devoted to the work of Alaïa, which captures the American market.

At last the international press is unanimous in its recognition of his talent.

1983   Charles Gallay opens an Alaïa boutique in Beverly Hills.

The *Alaïa* label spreads all over the world, notably in Barneys in New York, Chicago, Los Angeles and Tokyo; Neiman & Marcus in San Francisco; Les Créateurs in Geneva and above all in Joseph stores in London.

1985   Alaïa sets up at 17, rue du Parc-Royal in the Marais district, Paris, in what used to be an old inn. Andrée Putman is commissioned to do the decorations.

Alaïa continues with his low-cut designs. To emphasize the bust, he designs dresses with uplifted bustiers and puts his name to the 'stretch look' which he popularizes. The technology used is brought into the mainstream largely thanks to Alaïa.

During the winter of 1984–1985 the Museum of Contemporary Art in Bordeaux (the CAPC) devotes a retrospective fashion show to the designer.

In September, Jean-Paul Goude stages a fashion show at the Palladium in New York.

In October Alaïa receives two Fashion Oscars.

1988   Alaïa opens his own boutique in Soho, New York. The painter Julian Schnabel designs the décor in the style of a modern art gallery.

1990   Alaïa sets up in an old nineteenth-century warehouse right in the heart of the Marais district, at 7, rue de Moussy. Again Julian Schnabel is involved in the design.

1992   Alaïa launches his anti-stretch knit: 'Relax'.

1995   Stephanie Seymour celebrates her wedding at Alaïa's. Her dress, created for her by the designer, took 1,600 hours to make.

Azzedine Alaïa

The famous and revolutionary black leather tunic picked up by the press in 1981 which launched Alaïa internationally. Worn here by Leslie Weener. *Photo Toscani. © Marie-Claire.*
Drawing by Thierry Perez illustrating Alaïa's draped studded leather belt. It was one of the indispensable accessories of 1981, a decisive year for the designer.

Helena Christensen wearing a lace wrap over a black uplift bra and cotton satin hot-pants, with a wide jagged-edged leather belt with cut-out pattern. Summer 1992 collection. *© Photo all rights reserved.*
Hôtel du Nord style. Marie-Sophie Wilson wearing a matching bolero and shorts in mini hound's-tooth check over a white cotton blouse. Summer 1988 collection. *Photo Peter Lindbergh, March 1988.*

Drawing by Thierry Perez and photograph by André Rau, this long black chiffon dress with an inlaid 'tattoo' pattern from the 1987 collection was specially created for Naomi Campbell. It took six months to make and was a homage to both Madeleine Vionnet and Josephine Baker. When Naomi wore it for her first Alaïa fashion show, she also wore a helmet of moulded feathers. The designer never allowed the dress to be photographed on any other model. © Scoop/Elle TopModel (No. 3, January 1995).

In the heat of the night Alaïa becomes a tailor once again to finalize each of his prototypes by hand. On the right, the designer adjusts the width of a skirt for the Summer 1992 collection. *© Photo all rights reserved.*

These diabolo style belts, made of polished leather with a cut-out pattern and serrated edge, sit on top of one of Alaïa's two illuminated cabinets made of glass and steel. Designed by Sabino in the nineties, today they decorate the couturier's dining room. © *Photo all rights reserved.*
Elevated view of Alaïa's nineteenth-century steel and glass house in the heart of the Marais district, Paris. Under its glass roof Alaïa presents his collections and receives his friends. Here preparations are under way for a fashion show. *© Photo all rights reserved.*

Under a corset-style belt with three buckles a petticoat in broderie anglaise by Saint-Gall is worn over a pair of shorts in the same fabric. Summer 1992 collection. *© Photo all rights reserved.*
Sheath dress with bare back in jersey wool. This design, created for the Summer 1981 collection, was part of the first series which used zips with jersey, so that different parts of the body, such as the back, bust and hips, could be exposed as desired. Drawing by Thierry Perez.

Black skin: the miniaturization, using Latex, of a dress designed for Grace Jones for the Fashion Oscars in 1985. Thierry Perez created sculpted dolls for adults with some anatomical features resembling those of certain supermodels. © *Photo Marcel Hartmann.*
Grace Jones and Alaïa on stage at the Opéra in Paris for the Oscar presentation. *Photo Deutsh Horvais.* © Scoop – Paris Match.

Hooded cowl-neck dress in black jersey wool decorated with long zips. Autumn/Winter 1986–1987 collection. Drawing by Thierry Perez.
East meets west in this gossamer wedding dress made of cream georgette crêpe trimmed with three rows of gold and silver metal eyelets. This was one of a series of studded clothes presented as part of the Autumn/Winter 1986–1987 collection. © *Photo all rights reserved.*

The black 'Marseillaise'. Alaïa during the final fitting of the tricolour gown worn by the American opera singer Jessie Norman for the bicentenary celebrations of the French Revolution orchestrated by Jean-Paul Goude, 14 July 1989. *Photo P. Perrin.* © *Sygma.*

Wedding dress in stiffened tulle designed by Alaïa in 1988, worn here by Marie-Sophie. *Photo Peter Lindbergh.*
Eve Salvail wearing an overshirt in black chiffon decorated with cross motifs of the same material. This translucent garment is worn over a long white cotton poplin shirt. Summer 1993 collection. *Photo Jean-Baptiste Mondino.*

Safari jacket with patch pockets in beige cotton gabardine. Summer 1990 collection. Featured in *La Mode en peinture*, No. 16, June 1990. © *Photo all rights reserved.*
Bustier minidress in knitted string edged with a fringe of shells hanging up in the sunlit Marais studio. Summer 1990 collection. Featured in *La Mode en peinture*, No. 16, June 1990. © *Photo all rights reserved.*

'Tati' outfit: shorts, cap, jacket and bag in denim printed with the word 'Tati', inspired by the famous red and white hound's-tooth check of the Tati shop which has always been extremely popular in France due to its very low prices. Drawing by Thierry Perez.
The elegant supermodel Christy Turlington wearing the same design with a matching bra. Summer 1991 collection. *Photo Patrick Demarchelier.*

The essence of the Alaïa style. Two drawings by Thierry Perez whose ability to bring out the eroticism of the modern female form is ideally suited to the extreme femininity Alaïa looks for in some of his designs. Denim bra and shorts (left) with spiralling straps linking the thigh to the shoe. Summer 1991 collection. Matching bolero and skirt in black leather (right) with wide flesh-revealing bands strapped to the thigh with metal buckles. Autumn/Winter 1983–1984 collection.

Two beaded dresses, the one on the right in steel, drawn by Hélène Tran for *La Mode en Peinture*, No. 14, February 1989. © *Photo all rights reserved.*

Master craftsmanship was required for this chain mail – knotted and moulded by hand following the traditional technique of macramé – formerly used for soft furnishings – which Alaïa resurrects for this hooded bolero and mesh shorts with fitted lining fringed with beads. Between the stitches a scattering of sequins glint like dewdrops. Summer 1992 collection. © *Photo all rights reserved.*

Black-and-white striped cotton bustier over a long black leather skirt in waxed sheepskin, lacing up at the back. Summer 1992 collection. © *Photo all rights reserved.*

Artist and model: sitting on a metal Art Deco chair in Alaïa's boutique in front of a painting by the artist Julian Schnabel, Naomi Campbell is modelling a halter-neck top and high-leg shorts in guipure. Summer 1992 collection. *Photo A. Rau.* © Elle Top Model. **Photograph of Alaïa and Farida taken by Jean-Paul Goude in 1987.** This striking photograph – an optical illusion – made the cover of numerous magazines. © *Photo Jean-Paul Goude.*

A jumble of objects in a corner of Alaïa's studio, including this poster of the singer Tina Turner (photo taken in London by Michael Roberts in the eighties). A friend of Alaïa, Turner was the first star he designed clothes for – outfits for her performances as well as everyday – on a regular basis. **Dolls by Thierry Perez.** On the left, a full-length bustier dress made in strips of stretchy material (1985) and on the right, a knitted bustier in leopard print with matching boots and beret. Autumn/Winter 1991–1992 collection. © *Photo Marcel Hartmann.*

Wild beasts on the loose: a series of knitted leopard print garments created for the Autumn/Winter 1991–1992 collection. Standing in Alaïa's studio, from left to right: Tereza Maxova, Nadège, Beverly Peele, Deon Bray. Sitting, from left to right: Irene Pfeiffer, an unknown model, Gourmit, Carla Bruni, Yasmin Ghaury, Emma S., Helena Christensen and Claudia Mason. *Photo Jean-Baptiste Mondino.*

Some of the models who were to become famous during the nineties, modelling the black leopard print stretch lace catsuit with velvet inserts in Alaïa's studio. Autumn/Winter 1991–1992 collection. *Photo Jean-Baptiste Mondino.*

Group portrait to show the series of leather 'grillwork' designed by Alaïa for his Autumn/Winter 1991–1992 collection. The finely stitched leather has square metal links at its intersections and is worn over a Jacquard butterfly design slip and high-heeled boots in black buckskin. *Photo Jean-Baptiste Mondino.*

A drawing by the artist Thierry Perez, who frequently collaborated with Alaïa. An all-in-one bustier and hotpants in a Jacquard butterfly design, inspired by Arletty (right). Spring/Summer 1992 collection.
Photograph of Arletty from the film *Tempête.* Having become a friend of the great actress, the couturier was given the opportunity to design clothes for her. He always considered her natural elegance to be one of his main sources of inspiration.

Modes Gitanes. Photo of Alaïa by Jean-Paul Goude taken at the *Modes Gitanes* exhibition in 1994. Mercedes Metal, the flamenco dancer, is wearing a bustier dress decorated with black leather, which laces up at the back – the brightly coloured leather fringes of the underskirt can be seen through the strips.
Shoe with 'leg' heels in black patent leather, heel sculpted in resin, created for Alaïa by the bootmaker Raymond Massaro.

A collection of souvenirs which Alaïa keeps by him in his studio: Arletty in *Les Visiteurs du soir,* and signed photographs of Tina Turner, Naomi Campbell, Veronica Webb and various friends. On a hanger is a full-length sheath dress in stretch cotton with a low square neck edged with a Jacquard border and lace detail. Summer 1992 collection.
Long bustier dress in stretch lace. Drawing by Thierry Perez for the Summer 1993 collection.

The central aisles on two floors which form the heart of the building in the Marais, Paris, where the boutique, offices, studio and private apartments have all been brought together under one roof.
Naomi Campbell, one of the most famous supermodels in the world, was discovered by Alaïa when she was a teenager. She is wearing a bustier in bronze mosaic-patterned leather, black leggings and a monkey-style bolero in knitted plastic. Autumn/Winter 1994–1995 collection. *Photo André Rau for* Elle TopModel, *January 1995.*

Oriental and timeless. A full-length flowing gown in golden mesh on a glass torso created by the CIRVA of Marseilles. On the left, a detail showing the collar in tighter weave.

Acknowledgments

The publishers would like to thank Mr Azzedine Alaïa for the help he has given in the preparation of this book, as well as all those who contributed to this work, in particular: Naomi Campbell, Farida Khelfa, Grace Jones, Tina Turner, Jessie Norman, Jean-Paul Goude, Jean-Baptiste Mondino, Peter Lindbergh, Patrick Demarchelier, Julian Schnabel, Thierry Perez, Peter Knapp, Anne-Marie Perrier, Jean-Marie Perrier, Hélène Tran, Maïme Arnodin, Patrick Amselem, Mercedes Metal, Helena Christensen, Christy Turlington, Irène Pfeiffer, Claudia Mason, Beverly Peele, Yasmin Ghauri, Stephanie Roberts, Tereza Maxova, Deon Bray, Emma S., Gourmit, Marie-Sophie Wilson, Leslie Weener, Yannick Morisot, Marion de Beaupré, Brian Bantry, Vincent Simonet, Sebastien Roca, Auro Varani, Sabine Killinger, Raphael Fantin, Bruno Jamagne, Marilyn Gauthier, Jean-Marc Martinez, Cathy Queen, Sophie Theallet and Olivier Collinet.